Dinner's On...
15 Minutes Away

Woman's Day

Dinner's On...
15 Minutes Away

70 recipes that will save the day

filipacchi
publishing

Filipacchi Publishing
1633 Broadway
New York, NY 10019

© 2003 Filipacchi Publishing

Designed by Patricia Fabricant
Copyedited by Margaret Farley, Greg Robertson and
Kim Walker

ISBN 2-85018-661-9

Printed and bound in Italy

Contents

How many times have you heard the question, "What's for dinner?" *Woman's Day Dinner's On...* gives you 70 different answers. Once upon a time, the woman of the house was expected to slave over the stove for a good part of the day.

But times have changed. The trend now is to get something on the table that's not only quick and easy, but also nutritious and flavorful. All these recipes meet those requirements while giving new meaning to the term "fast food." Even gourmet cooks will appreciate our simple but satisfying meals. Add bread or a salad, an easy dessert, and it's dinner. Whatever you and your family crave, we have a fuss-free solution. Soups, salads, sandwiches, pasta, main-course dishes featuring chicken, pork, beef, fish: We show you how to whip up a good, satisfying meal in less time.

An added bonus to these easy-to-do meals: Many of them can be made ahead, then frozen or reheated—a boon for households where everyone comes and goes at different times. These meals also hold their own on family nights when everyone dines together. Plus, you get to sit down and enjoy more time at the table instead of sweating it out in the kitchen.

In the past, chefs wore the traditional toque or high hat. These days, the chef of the house wears many other hats as well: office worker, stay at home mom, college student, single parent. But everyone probably has one thing in common, and that's not having enough time in the day. Problem solved. With these recipes, that's one less worry in your life.

Italian Heroines

1 tsp oil, preferably olive
8 oz mushrooms, sliced (2 1/2 to 3 cups)
1 cup thinly sliced onion
4 hero (hoagie, sub) rolls, split
6 Tbsp reduced-fat basil pesto sauce
8 oz sliced cooked turkey
2 cups deli-style marinated roasted red and yellow bell peppers
1 cup (4 oz) preshredded mozzarella cheese

1 Heat oven to 425°F. Have a baking sheet ready.

2 Heat oil in a large nonstick skillet over medium-high heat. Add mushrooms and onion; sauté 5 to 7 minutes, stirring often, until lightly browned.

3 Meanwhile spread cut sides of rolls with pesto. Top with turkey and peppers, spoon on onion and mushrooms, and sprinkle with cheese.

4 Bake 5 minutes or until cheese melts.

SERVES 4

PER SERVING: 561 cal, 32 g pro, 51 g car, 5 g fiber, 26 g fat (8 g saturated fat), 71 mg chol, 971 mg sod

SPEED ZONE

Since most recipes include onions and peppers, slice or chop a bunch at a time and freeze them in ziptop freezer bags for fast use later.

DO IT...FAST

Clean as you go. Fill a large bowl or pan with hot soapy water so you can toss in cooking utensils as soon as you're done with them.

Cheddar, Pears and Watercress on Whole-Grain Bread

8 slices 7-grain sandwich bread
8 oz sharp yellow Cheddar cheese, sliced or
   coarsely shredded
1 ripe pear, cored, sliced very thin and gently tossed with
   1 tsp lemon juice
1 bunch watercress, picked over, rinsed and patted dry
   (1 1/3 cups)
1 Tbsp butter or margarine

1 Top 4 slices bread with half the cheese, the pear slices and watercress. Cover with remaining cheese and bread.

2 Melt half the butter in a large skillet over medium-low heat. Add sandwiches and cook until nicely browned on bottoms, about 5 minutes. Turn, add remaining butter, and cook 5 minutes longer or until underside is crisp and cheese melted. Remove to a cutting board; cut in half.

Ham and Eggplant Wraps

*4 burrito-size wraps, preferably spinach with garlic and pesto
  or sundried tomato (see Tip)*
1 jar (7 oz) roasted red peppers, well drained
12 oz thinly sliced ham
4 lettuce leaves
1 can (7 1/2 oz) caponata (eggplant appetizer)
SERVE WITH: potato chips and grapes

1 Warm wraps as directed on package. Meanwhile pat
roasted red peppers dry with paper towels and cut them
into narrow strips.

2 Lay ham and a lettuce leaf on lower third of each
wrap. Spoon on caponata; top with roasted pepper strips.

3 Tightly roll up from edge nearest you. Cut in half
diagonally before serving.

SERVES 4

PER SERVING: 406 cal,
  19 g pro, 40 g car, 5 g fiber,
  18 g fat (4 g saturated fat),
  48 mg chol, 1,891 mg sod

NOTE *A splash of vinegar on
the rolled-up wrap adds a
pleasant bite.*

TIP *Flavored burrito-size flour
tortillas are often called
wraps. Look for them in the
dairy or produce section of
your grocery.*

SERVES 4

PER SERVING: 459 cal,
31 g pro, 34 g car, 2 g fiber,
21 g fat (9 g saturated fat),
475 mg chol, 1,470 mg sod

NOTE *Good with bottled or deli pickled beets.*

TIP *All eight eggs can be added to the simmering water at one time.*

Eggs and Asparagus on a Raft

4 English muffins
1 lb thin asparagus
1 cup bottled light Parmesan Alfredo sauce
8 large eggs
8 thin slices baked ham (6 oz)
GARNISH: *chopped parsley*

1 Split and toast English muffins; place cut sides up on serving platter.

2 While muffins toast, half-fill a large nonstick skillet with water and bring to a boil over medium-high heat. Cut 1 in. off bottoms of asparagus. Add spears to skillet, reduce heat, cover and simmer 3 to 4 minutes until crisp-tender. Remove with tongs to a colander; keep water simmering.

3 Meanwhile heat Alfredo sauce in a small saucepan over medium-low heat or in microwave, stirring occasionally.

4 Break eggs into a bowl (see Tip) and slide into water in skillet. Cover and cook 5 to 6 minutes until whites set and yolks shake only slightly when pan is jiggled.

5 While eggs cook, place ham, then asparagus spears on muffin halves.

6 Using a slotted spoon, gently lift eggs from water and place 1 on each muffin half. Spoon sauce over eggs; sprinkle with parsley.

Red Pepper Quesadillas

Eight 8-in. flour tortillas
1 cup preshredded Cheddar cheese (4 oz)
1 cup frozen chopped red bell peppers, thawed
1/4 cup sliced scallions
1/4 cup chopped cilantro (optional)
4 tsp vegetable oil

1 Sprinkle 4 tortillas with 1/2 cup of the cheese, the red peppers, scallions and cilantro. Top with remaining 1/2 cup cheese and tortillas.

2 Heat 1 tsp oil in each of two nonstick skillets over medium heat. Cook a quesadilla in each about 2 minutes per side, turning once, until tortillas are crisp and cheese is melted; repeat with remaining quesadillas. Cut in wedges.

SERVES 4

PER SERVING: 391 cal,
13 g pro, 41 g car, 3 g fiber,
19 g fat (7 g saturated fat),
30 mg chol, 512 mg sod

NOTE *Next time you make bean soup, serve these Mexican "grilled cheese" sandwiches on the side.*

DO IT...FAST

Use kitchen scissors to cut open packages, snip herbs and trim fat off meat and poultry.

Savory Rollups

3 cups torn fresh spinach leaves, chopped
5 oz Monterey Jack or pepperjack cheese or a mix of both, shredded (1 1/4 cup)
1/2 a medium red bell pepper, cut in narrow strips
1/4 cup each sliced scallions and chopped cilantro
Four 7- to 8-in. flour tortillas

1 Mix spinach, cheese, bell pepper, scallions and cilantro in a medium bowl until combined.

2 Put each tortilla on a square of wax paper. Spoon equal amount of spinach mixture on each.

3 Microwave 1 at a time until cheese melts, about 30 seconds. Roll up tortillas, then cut them crosswise in quarters. Serve hot.

Tuna Wrap Sandwiches

1 can (6 oz) chunk light tuna in oil, drained
1/2 cup chopped celery
1/3 cup each chopped onion and pimiento-stuffed
  green salad olives
1/4 cup light mayonnaise
1/2 medium head iceberg lettuce, shredded (7 cups)
Four 8- to 9-in. burrito-size flour tortillas or wraps
1 cup preshredded Cheddar cheese (4 oz)
ACCOMPANIMENT: potato chips

1 Mix tuna, celery, onion, olives and mayonnaise in a medium bowl. Fold in lettuce.

2 Spoon about 1 1/2 cups tuna mixture down center of each tortilla; sprinkle 2 Tbsp cheese on either side of mixture.

3 Lightly coat a large nonstick skillet or griddle with nonstick spray. Cook each tortilla over medium heat about 2 minutes until underside is golden brown and cheese melts.

4 Fold tortilla in on 3 sides to enclose filling. Wrap in a paper napkin or wax paper to serve.

SERVES 4

PER SERVING: 394 cal,
  23 g pro, 26 g car, 3 g fiber,
  22 g fat (8 g saturated fat),
  42 mg chol, 890 mg sod

SERVES 4

PER SERVING: 454 cal,
32 g pro, 40 g car, 3 g fiber,
18 g fat (3 g saturated fat),
69 mg chol, 671 mg sod

TIP *Save the croutons from the salad mix for a snack or soup garnish.*

SERVES 4

PER SERVING: 424 cal,
21 g pro, 44 g car, 3 g fiber,
18 g fat (4 g saturated fat),
53 mg chol, 1,509 mg sod

Turkey Caesar Salad Wrap

1 bag (about 10 oz) Caesar-salad mix
12 oz thinly sliced cooked turkey
1 large tomato, cut in half, then thinly sliced
4 burrito-size flour tortillas

1 In a bowl, mix the lettuce, dressing and the cheese from salad mix (see Tip).

2 Lay turkey and tomato on lower third of each tortilla. Top with salad. Tightly roll up each one from edge nearest you. Cut in half to serve.

Curried Fruit and Ham Wrap

1/4 cup light mayonnaise
1 tsp curry powder
2 nectarines, thinly sliced
2 scallions, thinly sliced
1 rib celery, thinly sliced
12 oz thinly sliced ham
4 burrito-size flour tortillas
4 large red- or green-leaf lettuce leaves

1 Mix mayonnaise, curry powder, nectarines, scallions and celery in a bowl.

2 Lay ham on lower third of each tortilla. Top with nectarine mixture and lettuce. Tightly roll up each one from edge nearest you. Cut in half to serve.

SERVES 4

PER SERVING: 588 cal,
25 g pro, 55 g car, 3 g fiber,
30 g fat (11 g saturated fat),
96 mg chol, 1,375 mg sod

SERVES 4

PER SERVING: 484 cal,
14 g pro, 75 g car, 6 g fiber,
17 g fat (3 g saturated fat),
0 mg chol, 424 mg sod

Reuben Wrap

1/4 cup light mayonnaise
3 Tbsp each chili sauce, sweet pickle (India) relish and
   minced red onion
4 burrito-size flour tortillas
8 oz thinly sliced corned beef
4 oz thinly sliced Swiss cheese
16 oz prepared coleslaw

1 Mix mayonnaise, chili sauce, relish and minced onion in a small bowl.

2 Spread over lower third of each tortilla. Top with corned beef, cheese and coleslaw. Tightly roll up each one from edge nearest you. Cut in half.

Peanut Butter–Banana Wrap

2 bananas, halved lengthwise, then crosswise
1 cup seedless grapes, cut in half
2 tsp each honey and lemon juice
1/2 cup reduced-fat creamy peanut butter
4 burrito-size flour tortillas
3 medium carrots, shredded

1 Stir bananas, grapes, honey and lemon juice in a bowl to mix and coat.

2 Spread peanut butter over lower third of each tortilla. Top with carrots, then banana mixture. Tightly roll up each one from edge nearest you. Cut in half to serve.

Chickpea, Sprouts and Cheese Wrap

1 cup each *chopped seeded cucumber and rinsed canned*
  chickpeas (garbanzos)
1/2 cup *chopped tomato*
1 Tbsp each *olive oil and cider vinegar*
1/4 tsp each *salt and pepper*
1/2 cup *light garlic-and-herb spreadable cheese*
  (such as Alouette)
4 *burrito-size flour tortillas*
2 cups *mixed sprouts (about 1/2 a 3-oz pkg)*
12 *spinach leaves*

1 Mix cucumber, chickpeas, tomato, olive oil, cider
vinegar, salt and pepper in a bowl.

2 Spread cheese on lower third of each tortilla. Top with
sprouts, then chickpea mixture and spinach. Tightly roll up
each one from edge nearest you. Cut in half to serve.

SERVES 4

PER SERVING: 333 cal,
  12 g pro, 43 g car, 5 g fiber,
  13 g fat (4 g saturated fat),
  10 mg chol, 688 mg sod

Orange-Spinach Pasta

2 navel oranges
3/4 bunch scallions
1 cup fat-free half-and-half (such as Land O' Lakes)
12 oz capellini (angel-hair) pasta
2 bags (5 to 6 oz each) baby spinach

1 Bring 3 qts lightly salted water to a boil in a large covered pot over high heat.

2 Meanwhile finely grate peel from 1 orange and squeeze juice from both. Slice scallions (should be about 3/4 cup).

3 Bring orange juice and scallions to a simmer in a large nonstick skillet. Cook 3 minutes or until juice is reduced to about 1 Tbsp. Add half-and-half and grated orange peel. Simmer 1 minute, then remove skillet from heat.

4 Stir pasta into pot of boiling water. Cook, stirring often, 3 minutes. Stir in spinach and cook 1 minute more or until pasta is firm-tender. Drain in a colander and return to pot. Add orange sauce and toss to mix and coat.

SERVES 4

PER SERVING: 420 cal,
13 g pro, 85 g car, 7 g fiber,
1 g fat (0 g saturated fat),
0 mg chol, 507 mg sod

NOTE *Pass grated Parmesan cheese and crushed red pepper at the table.*

Angel-Hair Pasta with Tomato Cream Sauce

12 oz angel-hair pasta (capellini)
1 jar (14 oz) marinara sauce (about 1 2/3 cups)
3/4 cup frozen petite peas, not thawed
1/3 cup reduced-fat sour cream
GARNISH: chopped fresh basil and grated Parmesan cheese

1 Bring a covered large pot of lightly salted water to a boil. Add pasta and cook according to the directions on the package. Drain.

2 Meanwhile bring marinara sauce to a boil in a small saucepan over low heat. Stir in peas, cover and simmer 2 minutes or until peas are tender. Reduce heat to low, add sour cream and stir until blended.

3 Toss pasta with sauce. Top with basil.

SAUCE STAPLES

CANNED
- Tomatoes (whole, crushed, purée, sauce, paste, seasoned)
- Olives
- Tuna, salmon, sardines, clams
- Broth
- Caponata (eggplant appetizer)
- Beans (kidney, chickpeas, pinto)
- Mushrooms

BOTTLED
- Peppers (pickled and roasted)
- Bacon bits
- Marinated artichoke hearts
- Clam juice
- Basil pesto
- Dried tomatoes
- Olive oil

OTHER
- Dried herbs
- Fresh garlic (lots)
- Onions

THE EXTENDED PANTRY:

REFRIGERATOR
- Carrots
- Celery
- Parmesan cheese
- Cottage or ricotta cheese

FREEZER
- Vegetables (peas, broccoli, bell pepper and onion strips, assorted mixtures)

Pasta with Bolognese Sauce

1 lb bow-tie pasta (farfalle) or bellflower pasta (campanelle)
3 cups frozen green peas
8 oz lean ground beef
1 jar (26 oz) green-and-black-olive pasta sauce (puttanesca)
1 can (about 19 oz) chickpeas, rinsed

1 Cook pasta in a large pot of lightly salted water according to package directions, adding peas 3 minutes before pasta will be done. Drain; return to pot (off heat).

2 While pasta cooks, cook beef in a 3- to 4-qt saucepan over medium-high heat 3 to 4 minutes, breaking up clumps with a spoon. Drain off any fat. Add pasta sauce and chickpeas, bring to a boil, reduce heat, cover and simmer 4 minutes.

3 Pour over pasta. Toss to mix and coat.

SERVES 6

PER SERVING: 574 cal, 25 g pro, 85 g car, 10 g fiber, 14 g fat (4 g saturated fat), 23 mg chol, 1,191 mg sod

PICANTE PASTA *Bring tomato sauce to a boil. Stir in drained canned tuna in olive oil, capers, chopped pimiento-stuffed olives and a pinch each of dried oregano, basil and crushed red pepper. Simmer 5 minutes for flavors to blend.*

CLAMS CASINO *Sauté diced celery and minced garlic in olive oil until tender. Stir in bottled bacon bits and canned chopped clams with their juice. Heat through.*

PROVENÇAL *Bring to a boil canned crushed tomatoes, frozen bell pepper strips and onions, sliced black olives and canned chickpeas. Simmer until peppers are tender.*

PER SERVING: 472 cal,
17 g pro, 79 g car, 6 g fiber,
11 g fat (1 g saturated fat),
0 mg chol, 885 mg sod

PERFECT PASTA

- For each pound of pasta, bring 4 to 6 quarts of water to a rapid boil.

- Add 2 teaspoons salt, then stir in the pasta.

- Cook uncovered, stirring often the first 2 to 3 minutes, then stir every minute or so.

- Set a timer for the cooking time recommended on the package, but check for doneness toward the end by biting into a piece or strand. It should be tender but slightly firm at the center.

- Before draining, ladle off some of the cooking water and use it to make the finished dish a bit more saucy.

- Drain the pasta into a colander set in a sink with an open drain. Immediately return pasta to pot and toss with the sauce.

Fettuccine with Cilantro Pesto Sauce

1 lb fettuccine

PESTO
   2 cups each fresh cilantro and parsley
   1 can (4 oz) green chilies, drained
   1/3 cup unsalted roasted peanuts
   1/4 cup fresh lime juice
   2 Tbsp olive oil
   1 Tbsp bottled chopped garlic in oil
   1/2 tsp each ground cumin and salt
1 can (about 16 oz) black beans, rinsed
1 can (11 oz) Mexican-style corn, drained

1 Rinse the black beans and drain the corn in a colander. leave them there.

2 Cook pasta (see Perfect Pasta, left).

3 Meanwhile purée Pesto ingredients in food processor until smooth. With processor running, gradually add 1/3 cup pasta cooking water.

4 Drain pasta in the colander with beans and corn (so they can be warmed), return to pot and add Pesto and remaining ingredients. Toss to mix.

Pasta Rags and Warmed Salmon

6 qt water

2 Tbsp plus 1 tsp salt

1 lb fresh pasta sheets or 1 lb dry lasagna noodles

6 Tbsp extra-virgin olive oil

8 oz fresh salmon fillet, skin and bones removed,
  fish cut in paper-thin slivers

1 cup diced, seeded ripe tomato

1/4 cup chopped fresh dill

1/2 tsp pepper

1 Bring a large pot of salted water to a boil. Add pasta; cook 4 to 6 minutes until al dente (if using dry pasta, follow package directions). Drain, reserving 1 cup cooking water. Don't rinse pasta.

2 Put pasta in a bowl; add olive oil and toss to coat. Add 1 tsp salt and remaining ingredients; toss again, adding some of the reserved water if you prefer a more liquid sauce. Serve immediately.

SERVES 4

PER SERVING: 610 cal, 23 g pro, 66 g car, 3 g fiber, 29 g fat (4 g saturated fat), 33 mg chol, 528 mg sod

FYI *The heat of the pasta will cook the slivers of salmon.*

COOK IT...FAST

*Add cut broccoli, frozen cut
asparagus, green peas or mixed
vegetables to a pot of boiling
pasta 3 to 5 minutes before the
pasta will be done.*

Tuna Ribbons

8 oz (2 1/2 cups) sugar snap peas
1 large red bell pepper
2 medium lemons
1 box (8 oz) no-boil lasagna noodles
*2 cans (6 oz each) solid white tuna, packed in olive oil,
undrained*

1 Bring 8 cups water to boil in a large covered pot.

2 Meanwhile trim ends and strings from snap peas;
cut pepper in half, core and cut in narrow strips; and
squeeze lemons (you need 1/3 cup juice).

3 Add noodles to pot, cover and boil gently 5 minutes.
Add snap peas, cover and cook 2 to 3 minutes until peas
are tender and pasta is firm-tender.

4 Drain and place in a serving bowl. Add bell pepper
strips, lemon juice and undrained tuna; toss to mix and
coat. Serve immediately.

Fettuccine with Spinach and White Clam Sauce

1 box (12 oz) garlic-and-herb fettuccine
2 bags (10 oz each) washed spinach, tough stems removed
1 can (15 oz) white clam sauce with garlic and herbs
1/4 tsp crushed red pepper
1 can (14 oz) artichoke hearts, drained, cut in thirds
1 lemon, cut in wedges (see Tip)

1 Cook pasta in a large pot of lightly salted water according to package directions, adding spinach 1 minute before pasta will be done. Drain; return to pot (off heat).

2 Meanwhile simmer clam sauce and crushed pepper in a medium saucepan 3 to 5 minutes to develop flavor. Add artichoke hearts, pour over pasta, and toss to mix and coat. Serve with lemon wedges.

SERVES 4

PER SERVING: 471 cal, 21 g pro, 77 g car, 6 g fiber, 10 g fat (1 g saturated fat), 13 mg chol, 909 mg sod

TIP *The lemon wedges aren't just a garnish; a squeeze adds a special touch to this dish.*

SERVES 6

PER SERVING: 473 cal,
  26 g pro, 67 g car, 4 g fiber,
  10 g fat (2 g saturated fat),
  38 mg chol, 903 mg sod

FYI *Inexpensive canned pink salmon is a great protein value. Canning makes the bones soft and edible...a big calcium bonus, too.*

Salmon and Broccoli Pasta

1 lb spaghetti
2 Tbsp vegetable oil, preferably canola
1/2 cup plain fine dry bread crumbs
1 Tbsp minced garlic
1 cup chicken broth (from bouillon cubes)
1 bunch broccoli (1 1/4 lb), cut in small florets,
  stems peeled and sliced
1 can (14 3/4 oz) pink salmon (with juice, skin and bones),
  broken in chunks (see FYI)

1 Bring a large pot of lightly salted water to a boil, stir in spaghetti and cook as directed on package, until firm but tender.

2 While pasta cooks, heat 1 Tbsp oil in a large nonstick skillet over medium heat. Add bread crumbs and stir 1 to 2 minutes until evenly toasted. Remove to a bowl. Wipe skillet with paper towel.

3 Heat remaining 1 Tbsp oil in skillet. Add garlic and sauté 1 minute or until aromatic. Add broth and bring to a boil; add broccoli, reduce heat, cover and simmer 4 to 5 minutes until crisp-tender.

4 Drain pasta; return to pot. Add broccoli and broth, then salmon. Toss gently to mix. Serve with toasted bread crumbs at table, to be sprinkled on pasta in place of cheese.

SERVES 4

PER SERVING: 487 cal,
22 g pro, 63 g car, 2 g fiber,
17 g fat (9 g saturated fat),
67 mg chol, 1,479 mg sod

TIP A 4-oz can of diced green
chiles can be substituted for
the jalapeño peppers.

Tortelloni with Tex-Mex Tomato Cream Sauce

2 pkg (9 oz each) refrigerated mozzarella-garlic
  or other cheese tortelloni
1 Tbsp olive oil
1/2 cup sliced scallions
2 fresh jalapeño peppers, seeded and sliced (see Tip)
1 1/2 tsp minced garlic
1 can (16 oz) crushed tomatoes in purée
1/2 tsp salt
1/4 cup each 1/3-less-fat cream cheese (Neufchâtel)
  and chopped cilantro
GARNISH: chopped cilantro

1 Bring a large pot of lightly salted water to a boil. Add tortelloni; cook as package directs. Drain well; return to pot.

2 While pasta cooks, heat oil in a large nonstick skillet. Add scallions, jalapeños and garlic. Stir over medium heat 1 minute or until fragrant.

3 Stir in tomatoes and salt; bring to a simmer and simmer 1 minute or until slightly thickened. Add cream cheese; stir until cheese melts. Remove from heat and stir in cilantro.

4 Spoon tortelloni into serving bowls; top with sauce and garnish with cilantro.

Speedy Minestrone

2 cans (14 1/2 oz each) fat-free, 1/3-less-sodium chicken broth
2 cans (14 1/2 oz each) diced tomatoes with Italian herbs
1 box (10 oz) frozen green peas
1 cup uncooked elbow macaroni
2 cups very thinly sliced green cabbage
1 can (19 oz) white kidney beans (cannellini), rinsed

1 Bring broth and tomatoes to boil in a large saucepan.
2 Stir in frozen peas and macaroni and simmer 7 minutes or until tender.
3 Stir in cabbage and beans and cook 2 to 3 minutes until cabbage wilts. Thin with water if necessary.

SERVES 6

PER SERVING: 229 cal,
12 g pro, 43 g car, 7 g fiber,
1 g fat (0 g saturated fat),
0 mg chol, 861 mg sod

NOTE Let kids top the minestrone with cheese-flavored crackers; give adults grated Parmesan cheese.

PLANNING TIP Can be made up to 3 days ahead and refrigerated. Reheat in microwave or on stovetop, adding a little water if needed.

NOTE *Some like it hot, and if you do, shake on some hot pepper sauce.*

West African Peanut Soup

4 cups chicken broth (from bouillon cubes)
1 can (14 1/2 oz) stewed tomatoes
1 cup each chopped carrots and sliced scallions
3/4 cup reduced-fat peanut butter, smooth or chunky
1 cup 1% lowfat milk
1/4 cup instant mashed potato flakes

1 Bring broth, tomatoes, carrots and scallions to a boil in a 3-qt saucepan. Reduce heat and simmer 5 to 6 minutes until carrots are tender.

2 Stir in peanut butter until blended, then milk and potato flakes. Simmer 1 to 2 minutes to heat and thicken.

Tuscan Bread and Egg Soup

2 tsp olive oil
1 Tbsp minced garlic
5 cups chicken broth (from bouillon cubes)
1 can (15 oz) crushed tomatoes
2 cups frozen cut-leaf spinach
4 large eggs
Four 1-in.-thick slices toasted Italian bread
GARNISH: grated Parmesan cheese

1 Heat oil in a 3-qt saucepan. Add garlic and cook over medium-low heat 1 minute or until aromatic.

2 Stir in broth, tomatoes and spinach. Bring to a boil over medium heat. Reduce heat and simmer 5 minutes.

3 Gently break 1 egg into a cup; slide egg into soup. Repeat with remaining eggs. Let simmer 4 minutes without stirring.

4 Put 1 slice toast into each of 4 large soup bowls. Remove eggs with a slotted spoon and place 1 on each toast slice. Ladle soup into bowls. Sprinkle with Parmesan cheese.

SERVES 4

PER SERVING: 261 cal, 15 g pro, 31 g car, 4 g fiber, 9 g fat (2 g saturated fat), 213 mg chol, 1,749 mg sod

NOTE *This recipe is a good way to use up slightly dried-out Italian bread. Frozen green peas can be substituted for the spinach.*

TIP *Canned pumpkin isn't just for pie. It's a terrific source of vitamin A, and it gives this soup great creamy texture and winter-squash flavor, all with the ease of opening a can.*

Spicy Pumpkin Soup

1 tsp oil, preferably canola
1 Tbsp each minced garlic and chili powder
1/2 tsp ground cumin
4 cups chicken broth (from bouillon cubes)
1 can (19 oz) chickpeas, rinsed
1 can (15 oz) solid-pack pumpkin (see Tip)
1 cup corn kernels, canned or frozen
3/4 cup bottled medium-spicy salsa
GARNISH: preshredded Cheddar cheese, reduced-fat sour cream

1 Heat oil in a 3-qt saucepan. Add garlic, chili powder and cumin. Stir over medium-low heat 1 minute.

2 Add broth, increase heat, then stir in chickpeas, pumpkin, corn and salsa. Bring to a boil, reduce heat and simmer 10 minutes to develop flavors. Ladle into soup bowls; garnish with cheese and sour cream.

SERVES 4

PER SERVING: 102 cal,
  6 g pro, 17 g car, 2 g fiber,
  2 g fat (1 g saturated fat),
  5 mg chol, 735 mg sod

Cold Carrot Soup

3 1/2 cups frozen sliced carrots, thawed
1 cup chicken broth
1 tsp minced garlic
1/2 tsp ground cumin
2 cups buttermilk
1/2 tsp salt
GARNISH: chopped cilantro

Put carrots, broth, garlic and cumin in a food processor or blender and purée until smooth. Pour into a bowl. Add buttermilk and salt. To serve, sprinkle with chopped cilantro.

Spinach-Potato Soup

2 cans (14 1/2 oz each) roasted-garlic-seasoned chicken broth
3 cups frozen mashed potatoes (about half a 1-lb, 6-oz bag)
1 box (16 oz) frozen creamed spinach

1 Heat broth in a large pot; add potatoes and cook over medium-high heat, whisking occasionally, 5 minutes or until simmering and slightly thickened (see Tip).

2 Remove frozen spinach from pouch, add to potatoes, cover pot and simmer 8 to 10 minutes, whisking occasionally, until blended and spinach is heated through. (If soup is too thick, thin with hot water.) Pour into serving bowls; garnish if desired.

SERVES 4

PER SERVING: 225 cal,
6 g pro, 29 g car, 4 g fiber,
8 g fat (3 g saturated fat),
19 mg chol, 1,381 mg sod

TIP *For garnish, remove 1/4 cup hot mashed potatoes before adding spinach. Drop potatoes from tip of a spoon in parallel lines, then pull the tip of a knife across the lines, alternating direction between each pull.*

Hot and Sour Beef-Vegetable Soup

12 oz lean ground beef
2 pkg (3 oz each) beef-flavored ramen noodles
1 can (11 oz) baby corn "nuggets" (precut), drained
8-oz pkg sliced mushrooms (about 2 1/2 cups)
3/4 cup sliced red bell pepper
1/4 tsp black pepper
1 Tbsp each cider vinegar and soy sauce
1/4 cup sliced scallions
1/2 tsp dark Oriental sesame oil

1 Bring 4 cups water to a boil. Heat a large saucepan over medium-high heat. Add beef and cook, breaking up clumps, 3 minutes until no longer pink. Remove to a plate.

2 Add boiling water, the ramen noodle seasoning packets, corn, mushrooms and bell pepper to the pan. Bring to a boil, reduce heat and simmer uncovered 3 minutes or until pepper is crisp-tender.

3 Break noodles into saucepan, add black pepper, vinegar and soy sauce, and simmer 3 minutes or until noodles are tender. Stir in beef; heat through.

4 Remove from heat; stir in scallions and sesame oil.

SERVES 4

PER SERVING: 456 cal,
22 g pro, 33 g car, 3 g fiber,
26 g fat (11 g saturated fat),
64 mg chol, 1,095 mg sod

Italian Chicken Tenders with Squash

4 tsp olive oil
1 each medium zucchini and yellow summer squash
  (about 6 oz each), diced
1/4 cup Italian-seasoned dried bread crumbs
1 lb chicken tenders
1 1/2 cups bottled marinara sauce
1 can (4.75 oz) caponata (eggplant appetizer)
1/4 cup preshredded Italian cheese blend or mozzarella cheese
GARNISH: *chopped parsley*

1 Heat 2 tsp oil in a large nonstick skillet. Add zucchini and squash and sauté over high heat 2 minutes or until crisp-tender. Remove from pan.

2 Spread bread crumbs on wax paper; coat tenders with crumbs. Heat remaining 2 tsp oil in same skillet. Add chicken and cook over medium-high heat 2 minutes per side or until golden and cooked through. Remove from pan.

3 Return squash to skillet, stir in marinara sauce and caponata and bring to a simmer. Place tenders on top; sprinkle with cheese. Cover and cook over medium heat 1 minute or until cheese melts. Garnish with parsley.

SERVES 4

PER SERVING: 329 cal, 31 g pro, 20 g car, 5 g fiber, 13 g fat (2 g saturated fat), 71 mg chol, 1,060 mg sod

DOUBLE UP

Bread chicken or pork chops ahead of time. Freeze individually on a wax-paper-lined baking sheet until hard, pack with wax paper between layers and freeze up to 2 months. Thaw in refrigerator before panfrying.

NOTE *Serve with lime wedges and tortilla chips or warm flour tortillas.*

Fajita-Style Chicken Tenders with Corn and Black Beans

2 tsp olive oil
1 lb chicken tenders
1 pkt (1.12 oz) fajita seasoning mix
1 can (15 oz) black beans, rinsed
1 can (11 oz) whole kernel corn
1 cup salsa
3 Tbsp chopped fresh cilantro

1 Heat oil in a large nonstick skillet. Add tenders and cook over medium-high heat, turning once, 3 minutes or until lightly colored. Sprinkle with fajita seasoning and 2 Tbsp water; toss over medium heat 1 minute until coated and chicken is cooked through.

2 While tenders cook, combine beans, corn and salsa in a medium saucepan or microwave dish. Heat until hot. Remove from heat and stir in cilantro. Serve along with the tenders.

Sesame Chicken Fingers with Dipping Sauce and Onion Rice

ONION RICE
2 cups water
1 pkt onion soup mix (from a 2-oz box)
2 tsp butter or margarine
2 cups uncooked 5-minute rice
2 Tbsp sliced scallions

SESAME CHICKEN
1/2 cup sesame seeds
White from 1 large egg
1 lb chicken tenders
1 Tbsp oil

DIPPING SAUCE
1/2 cup red currant jelly, melted
3 Tbsp soy sauce
1 tsp grated fresh ginger

1 ONION RICE: Bring water, soup mix and butter to a boil in a medium-size skillet. Stir in rice and scallions, remove from heat, cover and let stand 5 minutes until liquid is absorbed and rice is tender.

2 SESAME CHICKEN: Meanwhile spread seeds on wax paper. Beat egg white in a shallow bowl with a fork. Coat tenders with egg white, then seeds.

3 Heat oil in a large nonstick skillet. Add tenders and cook over medium heat 2 minutes per side or until golden and cooked through.

4 DIPPING SAUCE: Whisk ingredients in a medium bowl until smooth. Spoon into small bowls.

5 Serve chicken with the sauce; serve rice on the side.

SERVES 4

PER SERVING: 591 cal, 35 g pro, 76 g car, 3 g fiber, 16 g fat (3 g saturated fat), 71 mg chol, 1,515 mg sod

DOUBLE UP

Cook a double amount of rice and freeze half in a microwavable container. To reheat, add a little water; nuke until hot.

PER SERVING: 459 cal,
41 g pro, 58 g car, 8 g fiber,
8 g fat (1 g saturated fat),
82 mg chol, 1,280 mg sod

TIP *If you end up with extra grated orange peel, freeze it for later use in cake, pancake or muffin batter.*

Orange-Scallion Chicken with Spinach and Couscous

2 Tbsp all-purpose flour
3/4 tsp salt
4 skinless, boneless chicken breast halves (about 5 oz each)
2 tsp vegetable oil
1 bag (10 oz) microwavable fresh baby spinach
1 box (5.6 oz) couscous with toasted pine nuts (pignoli)
1/3 cup golden raisins
2 navel oranges
2 Tbsp reduced-sodium soy sauce
1/3 cup sliced scallions

1 Mix flour and 1/2 tsp salt in a gallon-size plastic food bag. Add chicken, close bag and shake well to coat chicken evenly.

2 Heat oil in a large nonstick skillet over medium heat. Add chicken; cook 6 minutes, turning over once, until golden outside and barely pink in center.

3 While chicken cooks, microwave spinach as bag directs. Open bag; drain any liquid. Arrange spinach on serving plates, sprinkle with remaining 1/4 tsp salt and top with the chicken.

4 Meanwhile prepare couscous as package directs, adding raisins to cooking water with spice packet.

5 Grate peel from 1 orange (see Tip). Juice both oranges (1/2 cup). Mix 1 Tbsp peel, juice and soy sauce in the skillet. Gently boil 1 minute until slightly reduced. Add scallions; spoon over chicken and spinach. Serve with couscous.

Glazed Chicken with Couscous

One 1 1/2-lb rotisserie chicken, cut in quarters (see Tip)
1/4 cup apricot preserves
1 box (5.7 oz) herbed chicken-flavor couscous, with spice sack
1 bag (10 oz) fresh shredded carrots
2/3 cup golden raisins
1/3 cup sliced almonds
3 cups fresh baby spinach

1 Place oven rack in middle position. Heat broiler. Line a jelly-roll pan with foil (for easy cleanup), then lightly coat with nonstick cooking spray. Place chicken in pan, skin side up, and spread evenly with preserves.

2 Broil chicken on middle oven rack 8 to 10 minutes or until heated through.

3 Meanwhile place 2 1/2 cups water, spice sack, carrots and raisins in a large deep skillet. Cover and bring to a boil over high heat. Add couscous, return to a boil, then remove from heat. Cover and let stand 5 minutes.

4 While couscous stands and chicken broils, put almonds in a nonstick skillet over medium heat. Cook, stirring often, 3 minutes or until fragrant and golden.

5 Arrange spinach on platter; top with couscous and chicken. Sprinkle almonds over top.

SERVES 4

PER SERVING: 573 cal, 32 g pro, 75 g car, 8 g fiber, 20 g fat (5 g saturated fat), 102 mg chol, 1,063 mg sod

TIP *When buying the chicken, ask the deli clerk to cut it in quarters.*

PER SERVING: 320 cal,
32 g pro, 39 g car, 4 g fiber,
5 g fat (1 g saturated fat),
82 mg chol, 2,005 mg sod

TIP *You can also use leftover cooked chicken.*

Quick Chicken-and-Kielbasa Gumbo

*7 oz lowfat kielbasa (1/2 of a 14-oz package),
sliced 1/4 in. thick*

2 1/2 cups chicken broth

1 can (14 1/2 oz) Cajun stewed tomatoes

*1 1/2 cups frozen pepper stir-fry mixture (yellow, green and
red bell-pepper strips and onions)*

1 box (10 oz) frozen sliced okra, thawed

1 cup uncooked 5-minute rice

*1 box (10 oz) refrigerated skinless, fully cooked carved
chicken breast (such as Perdue), torn in shreds,
or 2 cups shredded cooked chicken (see Tip)*

ACCOMPANIMENT: jalapeño pepper sauce on the side

1 Cook kielbasa in a 3-qt saucepan over medium-high heat, stirring often, until lightly browned, about 3 minutes.

2 Add broth, tomatoes and stir-fry mixture. Cover and bring to a boil over high heat. Add okra and simmer 3 minutes. Stir in rice.

3 Cover and simmer 1 to 2 minutes or until vegetables and rice are tender. Stir in chicken and serve.

Thai Peanut-Pork Stir-Fry

2 tsp vegetable oil

12 oz pork tenderloin, trimmed of visible fat and thinly
sliced crosswise

2 cloves garlic, thinly sliced

3 1/2 cups broccoli florets (from a 16-oz bag)

1 medium red bell pepper, halved, seeded and cut lengthwise
in 1/2-in.-wide strips

1 can (14 oz) reduced-fat and -calorie (lite) coconut milk
(see Tip)

1 packet (3 1/2 oz) peanut-sauce mix (see Tip)

1 cup uncooked 5-minute white rice

1 Heat the vegetable oil in large nonstick skillet. Add the
pork and garlic and stir-fry 2 to 3 minutes until cooked
through. Place on plate.

2 To skillet, add broccoli, red pepper, coconut milk and
peanut-sauce mix. Bring to boil; reduce heat, cover and simmer 6 minutes until vegetables are crisp-tender.

3 Meanwhile, cook rice according to package directions.
Return pork and garlic to skillet and simmer a few minutes
until sauce thickens slightly. Serve with rice.

SERVES 4

PER SERVING: 402 cal,
27 g pro, 45 g car, 6 g fiber,
14 g fat (6 g saturated fat),
55 mg chol, 496 mg sod

TIP If you can't find reduced-
fat coconut milk or peanut-
sauce mix in your supermar-
ket, call A Taste of Thai at
800-243-0897 for a store
near you that carries their
products or for their mail-
order catalog.

SERVES 4

PER SERVING: 286 cal,
20 g pro, 28 g car, 6 g fiber,
11 g fat (5 g saturated fat),
73 mg chol, 340 mg sod

SPEED ZONE

Substitute cutlets in recipes that call for boneless chicken breasts or pork chops. They'll cook in less than half the time.

Sweet and Sour Pork Cutlets with Vegetables

2 Tbsp all-purpose flour
4 pork cutlets (about 12 oz)
2 Tbsp stick butter or margarine
2 bags (5 oz each) baby spinach
1 cup shredded carrots (from a 10-oz bag)
3/4 cup orange juice
1/4 cup dried cranberries or raisins
1 Tbsp each brown sugar and Dijon mustard

1 Put flour in a large plastic ziptop bag. Add cutlets, seal bag and shake to coat.

2 Heat 1 Tbsp butter in a large nonstick skillet. Add cutlets and cook 3 minutes, turning over once, until lightly browned and cooked through. Remove to a plate.

3 While cutlets cook, put spinach and carrots in a large microwave-safe bowl. Cover and microwave on high about 3 1/2 minutes, tossing once, until tender.

4 Add remaining ingredients to skillet. Stir to combine, bring to a boil, reduce heat and simmer 2 minutes. Remove from heat, stir in remaining butter and pour over cutlets. Serve with spinach and carrots.

Sausage and Peppers

8 oz each hot and sweet Italian sausage, sliced 1 in. thick
1 each large red and green bell pepper, cored, seeded and cut in
* 1/2-in.-wide strips*
1/4 cup water
8 oz crusty Italian or French bread
2 cans (14 1/2 oz each) diced tomatoes in juice, drained

1 Put sausage, peppers and water in a large, deep skillet. Cover and bring to a boil over high heat. Reduce heat slightly, cover and boil gently 4 minutes or until sausage is cooked through and peppers are tender.

2 Meanwhile cut bread in twelve 1/2-in.-thick slices.

3 Drain off sausage and pepper and discard pan drippings. Add tomatoes and cook, uncovered, over high heat 2 minutes until tomatoes are hot. Serve on, or with, the bread.

SERVES 4

PER SERVING: 476 cal,
24 g pro, 42 g car, 4 g fiber,
24 g fat (8 g saturated fat),
65 mg chol, 1,431 mg sod

NOTE *Serve with steamed broccoli. For a reduced-calorie version, use turkey sausage.*

NOTE *You can replace the pork with chicken or turkey.*

TORTILLAS WITH SCALLION BUTTER

Mix **2 Tbsp softened butter, 1 Tbsp chopped scallions, 1/4 tsp ground cumin** and **a pinch *each* salt and pepper.** Spread on 1 side of **4 taco-size flour tortillas;** fold each in quarters. Place on a microwave-safe plate, cover with wax paper and microwave 1 minute until warm (the tortillas can be heated in the oven).

Creamy Santa Fe Cutlets

3 Tbsp all-purpose flour
1/4 tsp salt
1/8 tsp pepper
1 lb 1/4-in.-thick pork cutlets
3 tsp oil
1/2 cup salsa
1/2 cup frozen corn
1/4 cup water
1/4 cup reduced-fat sour cream
1/4 cup chopped cilantro
ACCOMPANIMENTS: *green salad with sliced cucumbers, halved cherry tomatoes and baby carrots*

1 Combine flour, salt and pepper; dredge pork cutlets in flour mixture.

2 Heat 2 tsp oil in a nonstick skillet. Sauté half the cutlets 1 1/2 minutes per side until cooked. Remove to a plate. Repeat with remaining oil and cutlets. Cover to keep warm.

3 After removing cutlets from skillet, add salsa, frozen corn and water. Simmer 1 minute. Off heat, stir in reduced-fat sour cream and chopped cilantro.

Ham-and-Vegetable Frittata

1 bag (16 oz) frozen mixed vegetables (broccoli, corn and
   red peppers, see Tip)
6 large eggs
8 oz sliced baked Virginia ham
1 Tbsp vegetable oil
3/4 cup shredded Cheddar cheese
ACCOMPANIMENT: crusty French or Italian bread

1 Heat broiler. Bring 1/3 cup water to a boil in a covered large nonstick skillet.

2 Add frozen vegetables to skillet, cover and cook over
high heat 3 minutes.

3 Meanwhile whisk eggs in a bowl. Stack sliced ham
and cut in narrow strips.

4 Drain vegetables in a colander; wipe skillet dry.

5 Heat oil in skillet, add eggs and sprinkle with ham,
vegetables and cheese. Cover and cook over medium-low
heat 6 minutes or until eggs are set on the bottom, but
still slightly wet on the top.

6 Broil 4 to 5 in. from heat source (see Note) 1 to 2
minutes until top is set and golden. Slide onto serving
plate, cut in wedges and serve with bread.

SERVES 4

PER SERVING: 394 cal,
   33 g pro, 14 g car, 2 g fiber,
   23 g fat (9 g saturated fat),
   381 mg chol, 1,770 mg sod

TIP You can substitute any
   16-oz bag of frozen mixed
   vegetables you like for the
   mixture described.

NOTE If the skillet's handle is
   plastic or wood, double-wrap
   it in foil to protect it from
   scorching under the broiler.

NOTE *Buy bags of preshredded carrots, cabbage and broccoli. In only a few minutes, they can be sautéed or steamed in a covered skillet with just a little water or broth.*

Beef with Peanut Sauce

2 cups uncooked 5-minute rice
1 Tbsp vegetable oil
12 oz top round beef steak, cut diagonally in thin slices against the grain
1/3 cup bottled Thai peanut sauce
1 bag (16 oz) refrigerated broccoli coleslaw mix (shredded broccoli, carrots and red cabbage)

1 Bring 2 cups water to boil in a medium saucepan. Stir in rice, cover, remove from heat and let stand.

2 Heat oil in a large nonstick skillet over medium-high heat. Add beef and stir-fry 30 to 45 seconds until barely pink. Remove to a bowl and stir in peanut sauce.

3 Put slaw mix and 1/4 cup water in skillet. Cook, stirring 3 to 4 minutes, until vegetables are crisp-tender.

4 Add beef mixture to vegetables and stir 1 minute or until hot. Serve over rice.

SERVES 4

PER SERVING: 349 cal,
 24 g pro, 27 g car, 3 g fiber,
 16 g fat (5 g saturated fat),
 68 mg chol, 864 mg sod

TIP *If you don't have Cajun
seasoning, use chili powder.*

Cajun Steak and Fries

1 lb boneless sirloin steak
2 tsp Cajun seasoning (see Tip)
3 cups frozen steak fries
1 medium onion, sliced
Nonstick cooking spray
1 Tbsp steak sauce

1 Heat broiler and spray broiler-pan rack with non-stick cooking spray. Rub steak with Cajun seasoning and place on prepared rack.

2 Spread fries and onion around steak; coat onion with cooking spray. Broil 7 minutes, remove onion, turn steak and fries over and broil 5 minutes longer or until steak is lightly charred (it will be medium-rare) and fries are crisp.

3 Slice steak, drizzle with sauce and top with onion.

Unstuffed Peppers

2 cups uncooked instant (10-minute) brown rice
12 oz lean ground beef
1 tsp olive oil
1 each red and yellow bell pepper, cored and cut in strips
2 cups bottled marinara sauce
1 tsp fennel seeds (optional)
1/2 cup shredded mozzarella cheese

1 Bring 1 3/4 cups water to boil in a medium saucepan. Add rice, cover and simmer 5 minutes. Remove from heat; let stand until ready to serve, at least 5 minutes.

2 Meanwhile heat a large nonstick skillet over medium-high heat. Add ground beef and cook, breaking up clumps with a wooden spoon, about 3 minutes or until meat is no longer pink. Remove to a plate and set aside.

3 Heat oil in skillet. Add peppers and sauté over high heat 3 minutes or until lightly charred in a few places. Add sauce and fennel seeds, bring to a simmer, cover and cook 3 minutes or until peppers are tender.

4 Stir in beef; heat through. Spoon rice on serving plates, top with beef mixture and sprinkle with cheese.

SERVES 4

PER SERVING: 531 cal,
24 g pro, 53 g car, 4 g fiber,
28 g fat (10 g saturated fat),
75 mg chol, 918 mg sod

DOUBLE UP

Make a basic ground-meat mixture and use half for meat loaf, the remainder for meatballs. Bake side-by-side along with potatoes. Add meatballs to bottled pasta sauce and freeze; serve meat loaf with the potatoes.

PER SERVING: 579 cal,
27 g pro, 52 g car, 3 g fiber,
30 g fat (10 g saturated fat),
85 mg chol, 1,078 mg sod

TIP *Corn toaster cakes may be
substituted for corn muffins.*

Barbecue Beef on Corn Muffins

1 lb lean ground beef
1 can (14 1/2 oz) diced tomatoes in juice
1 can (11 oz) Mexican-style corn, drained
1/2 cup bottled barbecue sauce
1 1/2 tsp chili powder
4 purchased corn muffins, cut in half (see Tip)
1/3 cup chopped cilantro

1 Heat a large nonstick skillet over medium-high heat. Add ground beef and cook, breaking up clumps with a wooden spoon, 3 minutes or until no longer pink.

2 Add remaining ingredients except muffins and cilantro to meat in skillet, bring to a simmer and cook uncovered 5 minutes to develop flavors.

3 Meanwhile heat broiler and place muffins cut sides up on a baking sheet. Broil 1 to 2 minutes until lightly toasted.

4 Stir cilantro into beef mixture; remove from heat. Spoon mixture over toasted muffins.

Quick Lamb Stew with Rice

12 oz ground lamb (see Tip)
1 Tbsp minced garlic
1 tsp ground cumin
1/2 tsp each dried oregano, ground cinnamon and salt
1 can (15 oz) tomato sauce
2 each medium zucchini and yellow summer squash,
  cut in 1/2-in.-wide half-rounds
1 jar (15 oz) whole small onions, drained
2 cups uncooked 5-minute rice
GARNISH: pitted kalamata olives

1 Cook lamb, garlic, cumin, oregano, cinnamon and salt in a large nonstick skillet over medium-high heat, breaking up clumps of meat with a spoon, 3 minutes or until meat is no longer pink.

2 Stir in tomato sauce, 1/3 cup water, the squashes and onions. Cover, bring to a boil, reduce heat and simmer 10 minutes or until squashes are tender.

3 Meanwhile cook rice as package directs. Serve stew over rice; garnish with olives.

SERVES 4

PER SERVING: 507 cal,
  22 g pro, 59 g car, 5 g fiber,
  21 g fat (9 g saturated fat),
  62 mg chol, 1,386 mg sod

TIP Ground beef, turkey or chicken can be substituted for the lamb.

SERVES 4

PER SERVING: 315 cal,
40 g pro, 6 g car, 0 g fiber,
13 g fat (2 g saturated fat),
110 mg chol, 145 mg sod

BROCCOLINI WITH GARLIC

Bring 4 cups water to a boil in a large nonstick skillet. Add **2 bunches broccolini (about 1 lb) ends trimmed**; reduce heat, cover and simmer 6 minutes or until crisp tender. Drain in a colander. Heat **1 tsp of olive oil** in same skillet. Add **1 large clove garlic sliced** and cook over low heat 1 minute or until light golden. Add broccolini, **1/4 tsp** *each* **salt and pepper**, toss to mix and coat.

SERVES 4

PER SERVING: 60 cal,
4 g pro, 9 g car, 1 g fiber,
1 g fat (0 g saturated fat),
0 mg chol, 178 mg sod

Asian Broiled Salmon

1/4 cup each bottled stir-fry sauce and orange juice
2 Tbsp chopped cilantro
Four 1-in.-thick salmon steaks (8 oz each)

1 Heat broiler. Line broiler pan with foil (for easy cleanup) and coat broiler-pan rack with nonstick spray.

2 Mix stir-fry sauce, orange juice and cilantro in a small bowl. Remove and reserve 3 Tbsp for the cooked fish.

3 Brush both sides of salmon with sauce; place on prepared rack. Broil 5 minutes; turn fish over and brush with sauce again. Broil 3 minutes longer or until the fish is just opaque at center when tested with tip of a knife. Drizzle with the reserved sauce.

Broiled Catfish with Grape Sauce

4 farm-raised catfish fillets (4 to 5 oz each)
1 lemon
1/2 tsp each salt and pepper
1 bag (1 lb) frozen stir-fry vegetables
1 pkg (2 lb) refrigerated mashed potatoes (see Tip)

GRAPE SAUCE
  1 bunch scallions
  1 tsp vegetable oil
  1 1/2 tsp cornstarch
  1 cup Italian herb-seasoned chicken broth (see FYI)
  1 1/2 cups seedless red grapes

1 Heat broiler. Line a rimmed baking sheet with foil (for easy cleanup), then lightly coat with nonstick cooking spray.

2 Place fish, skin side down, in prepared pan. Cut lemon in 4 wedges; squeeze on fish. Season with salt and pepper.

3 Broil fillets 4 to 5 in. from heat source 8 to 10 minutes, until opaque at thickest part.

4 Meanwhile, following directions on each package, cook vegetables on stovetop and heat potatoes in microwave.

5 GRAPE SAUCE: Thinly slice white part of scallions (see Note). Put a large nonstick skillet over medium-high heat. Add oil and scallions; sauté 1 minute. Whisk cornstarch into broth, then whisk both into skillet. Simmer uncovered about 2 minutes until slightly thickened. Cut grapes in half, add to sauce and heat through.

6 Transfer fish to platter. Stir drippings into Sauce; spoon on fish. Serve with mashed potatoes and vegetables.

SERVES 4

PER SERVING: 456 cal, 28 g pro, 54 g car, 6 g fiber, 14 g fat (2 g saturated fat), 43 mg chol, 1,199 mg sod

TIP For quick mashed spuds from scratch, cut 4 peeled medium potatoes in 1-in. cubes. Microwave in bowl covered with vented plastic wrap (no water needed) 8 minutes or until soft. Mash as usual.

FYI Canned seasoned chicken broth comes in 2 flavors: Italian herb and roasted garlic. Use it in place of water or plain broth to enhance the flavor of a dish.

NOTE Garnish by slicing the green part of the scallions diagonally and sprinkling them over the fish.

TIP *The Creole seasoning on the bread is quite spicy. Use less if serving children or folks who like their food on the tame side.*

Shrimp and Corn Broiler Dinner

4 ears of corn in husks (no need to remove silk)
1 lb raw large shrimp, unshelled
1/2 cup bottled barbecue sauce
1 tsp dried thyme
1 long loaf (8 oz) Italian bread, cut in half lengthwise
2 Tbsp vegetable oil
1 1/2 tsp Creole seasoning or chili powder (see Tip)

1 Remove broiler pan with broiler-pan rack from oven. Position 1 oven rack close to broiler. Heat broiler.

2 Use kitchen scissors to cut off husk and silk extending from end of ears of corn to keep them from burning.

3 Put corn directly on oven rack and broil 2 minutes, turning ears over once (husks will scorch—that's OK). Meanwhile toss shrimp, barbecue sauce and thyme in a medium bowl to mix and coat.

4 Using tongs, turn corn and transfer to broiler-pan rack; add shrimp in a single layer. Broil 4 minutes, turning corn after 2 minutes. Turn shrimp and corn over and broil 3 minutes longer or until corn is tender and shrimp are cooked through. Remove to a serving platter.

5 Meanwhile brush cut sides of bread with oil and sprinkle with Creole seasoning. Place on broiler-pan rack and broil until toasted, about 1 1/2 minutes.

6 To serve: Holding hot corn with a kitchen towel, remove husk and silk (they'll come off easily). Cut bread in 3-in. pieces. Have diners peel their own shrimp.

Quick Shrimp-and-Kielbasa Paella

1 tsp vegetable oil
1 medium onion, thinly sliced
1 tsp ground turmeric
1/2 tsp salt
1/8 to 1/4 tsp crushed red pepper
1 can (14 1/2 oz) roasted-garlic seasoned chicken broth
    (see Tip)
1 can (14 1/2 oz) diced tomatoes
2 cups frozen petite peas
8 oz medium raw shrimp, peeled and deveined
8 oz 2/3-less-fat turkey kielbasa
2 cups instant long-grain white rice

1 Heat a large deep skillet over medium-high heat. Add oil and onion to skillet and sauté 1 minute until onion softens.

2 Stir in turmeric, salt and crushed pepper, then chicken broth, tomatoes and frozen peas. Increase heat to high, cover and bring to a boil.

3 Add shrimp, kielbasa and rice. Stir to mix all ingredients. Cover and return to a boil. Remove from heat; let stand 5 minutes before serving.

SERVES 4

PER SERVING: 441 cal, 29 g pro, 63 g car, 8 g fiber, 8 g fat (3 g saturated fat), 101 mg chol, 1,621 mg sod

TIP Canned seasoned chicken broth comes in 2 flavors: Italian herb and roasted garlic. Use it in place of water or plain broth to enhance the flavor of a dish.

TIP *Buy ready-to-heat garlic
bread in the bread aisle or
bakery section of your super-
market or grocery.*

Italian Fillet Skillet

1 loaf (8 oz) garlic bread (see Tip)
1 medium onion
5 small or 2 medium zucchini (1 lb)
1 can (14 oz) diced Italian-seasoned tomatoes
*1 lb small fresh fish fillets (such as tilapia, turbot or
red snapper), no more than 1/2 in. thick*

1 Place bread halves, seasoned side up, on a baking
sheet. Place in oven and heat to 425°F.

2 Lightly coat a large nonstick skillet with nonstick
cooking spray. Heat over medium-high heat. Thinly slice
onion; spread over bottom of skillet.

3 While onion cooks, cut small zucchini in 1/2-in.-thick
rounds or cut medium-size in half lengthwise, then crosswise in 1/2-in.-thick half-rounds. Stir into onions along with
half the tomatoes. Bring to a boil.

4 Lay fish fillets in a single layer on top of the vegetables. Pour remaining tomatoes over fish. Cover and cook 7
to 8 minutes until fish is cooked through and zucchini is
crisp-tender.

5 Remove bread from oven. Cut each half in 4 pieces.

Greek Shrimp Kabobs
with Feta Bread

1 lb large raw shrimp, peeled
1 medium zucchini, cut in 16 bite-size chunks
8 cherry tomatoes
1/4 cup bottled vinaigrette dressing
1 loaf French bread
Garlic-flavor nonstick seasoning spray
1/2 tsp dried oregano
1/2 cup crumbled feta cheese

1 Heat broiler and spray broiler-pan rack with garlic-flavor nonstick seasoning spray.

2 In a bowl toss shrimp, zucchini, tomatoes and vinaigrette dressing; let stand 5 minutes.

3 Meanwhile cut bread in half lengthwise, then cut each half in 4 pieces. Coat with garlic-flavor spray, then sprinkle with oregano and feta cheese.

4 Thread shrimp and vegetables on eight 10-in. skewers (see Note) and place on prepared rack. Broil 3 minutes, turn kabobs over and add bread to pan. Broil 2 minutes until shrimp are cooked through and bread is golden.

SERVES 4

PER SERVING: 381 cal, 31 g pro, 35 g car, 2 g fiber, 12 g fat (4 g saturated fat), 188 mg chol, 925 mg sod

NOTE *Shrimp and vegetables can also be broiled without being skewered.*

TIP *Love the taste of olive oil? Buy a small bottle of extra-virgin and mix it with a flavorless, less expensive oil like canola. The olive flavor comes through for half the price.*

Shrimp with Spinach and Cherry Tomatoes

1 Tbsp olive oil (see Tip)
1 lb medium-size shrimp, peeled and deveined (about 27)
1/2 tsp salt
1/8 tsp crushed red pepper
2 medium-size cloves garlic, peeled
2 bags (10 oz each) prewashed spinach
1 pint (2 cups) cherry tomatoes, red and/or yellow, preferably small
ACCOMPANIMENTS: orzo (rice-shaped pasta) or angel-hair (capellini) pasta tossed with olive oil and Parmesan cheese

1 Put oil in a large, heavy skillet over high heat. Add shrimp, salt and crushed pepper. Squeeze garlic through a garlic press over shrimp mixture. Stir to mix.

2 Cook 2 minutes, stirring often, until shrimp just start to turn pink.

3 Stir in about 1/3 the spinach and all the tomatoes. Cook 1 minute, tossing often with 2 large spoons, until spinach starts to wilt. Stir in half the remaining spinach and cook 1 minute until wilted. Add remaining spinach and cook 1 minute longer until all spinach is wilted, cherry tomatoes are hot and shrimp are cooked through.

8-Minute Scallop Sauté

2 Tbsp butter
1/2 tsp minced garlic
1 lb sea, bay or calico scallops
2 cups coarsely chopped ripe tomatoes
1/4 tsp salt
2 Tbsp chopped parsley
ACCOMPANIMENTS: broccoli, rice and lemon wedges

1 Melt 1 Tbsp butter in a medium-size skillet. Add garlic and cook over low heat 1 minute.

2 Stir in scallops, tomatoes and salt. Cover and cook 2 to 4 minutes, stirring once or twice, until scallops are opaque at centers. Stir in remaining butter.

3 Remove from heat and stir in parsley.

SERVES 4

PER SERVING: 171 cal, 20 g pro, 7 g car, 1 g fiber, 7 g fat (4 g saturated fat), 53 mg chol, 393 mg sod

Curried Vegetable Stew

1 can (14 oz) lite coconut milk
1 Tbsp curry powder
1 tsp salt
1/8 tsp ground red pepper (cayenne)
1 medium onion
1 large sweet potato
1 medium red bell pepper
1 bag (20 oz) frozen cauliflower
1 bag (1 lb) frozen baby bean and carrot blend
ACCOMPANIMENT: pita or crusty bread

1 Place a large pot over medium-high heat. Add coconut milk, curry powder, salt and ground pepper. Stir to mix. Cover; bring to a boil.

2 Meanwhile peel sweet potato and cut lengthwise; halve onion crosswise. Using the slicing disk of a food processor, thinly slice the onion and potato. Coat a skillet with nonstick cooking spray; add onion and potato and sauté 1 to 2 minutes until onion softens.

3 Add onion and potato to large pot with coconut mixture and cook 2 minutes. Meanwhile halve and seed bell pepper and cut in 1-in. pieces.

4 Add bell pepper to pot along with frozen vegetables. Bring to a boil and cook 7 minutes or until tender.

SERVES 4

PER SERVING: 224 cal, 7 g pro, 38 g car, 10 g fiber, 6 g fat (3 g saturated fat), 0 mg chol, 687 mg sod

Vegetarian Chili

2 cups uncooked instant (10-minute) brown rice

2 cans (10 oz each) diced tomatoes and green chiles

1 can (about 19 oz) black beans, rinsed

1 box (10 oz) frozen corn and roasted red peppers
  (Southwestern style)

1/4 cup tomato paste

3 Tbsp fresh lime juice

TOPPINGS (optional): reduced-fat sour cream and chopped
  cilantro

1 Cook rice as directed on package. Remove from heat, stir, then cover and let stand 5 minutes.

2 Meanwhile heat remaining ingredients in a covered saucepan, stirring occasionally, 8 minutes or until slightly thickened.

3 Fluff rice with a fork. Serve with chili and Toppings.

Middle Eastern Chickpeas with Couscous

2 large red potatoes, cut in 3/4-in. pieces
1 medium zucchini (about 8 oz), cut in 3/4-in. pieces
1 cup chicken or vegetable broth
1/2 tsp ground cumin
1/4 tsp each ground cinnamon, salt and pepper
1 box (10 oz) couscous (1 1/2 cups)
1 cup packed cilantro leaves
1 can (15 to 16 oz) chickpeas (garbanzo beans),
  drained and rinsed
1 can (7 1/2 oz) caponata (eggplant appetizer)
1/2 cup plain lowfat yogurt
GARNISH: cilantro sprigs

1 Bring potatoes, zucchini, broth, cumin, cinnamon, salt and pepper to a boil in a medium skillet. Reduce heat and simmer 8 to 10 minutes until potatoes are tender.

2 Meanwhile cook couscous according to package directions and coarsely chop the cilantro.

3 When potatoes are tender, add the cilantro, chickpeas and caponata to skillet mixture. Cook just to heat through.

4 Place couscous on a serving platter. Add vegetable mixture. Top with dollops of yogurt. Garnish with cilantro.

SERVES 4

PER SERVING: 454 cal,
  18 g pro, 80 g car, 13 g fiber,
  7 g fat (1 g saturated fat),
  2 mg chol, 782 mg sod

Mexican Caesar Salad

2 bags (7.5 oz each) complete Caesar salad with fat-free
  dressing and croutons (see Tip)
2 tsp ground cumin
1 can (19 oz) black beans, rinsed
1 pt cherry tomatoes, cut in half
4 cups (2 oz) baked tortilla chips, broken in bite-size pieces
  (2 cups)

1 Squeeze salad dressing from pouches into a small
bowl; stir in cumin.

2 Put salad greens from both bags, the beans and cherry tomatoes in a salad bowl.

3 Add dressing and toss to mix and coat. Scatter tortilla
chips on top.

SERVES 4

PER SERVING: 236 cal,
  9 g pro, 42 g car, 7 g fiber,
  2 g fat (0 g saturated fat),
  0 mg chol, 757 mg sod

TIP *Use the croutons as a
snack, or sprinkle them on
tomato or split-pea soup.*

TIP *Look in your market's produce section for pineapple
with the peel and core
removed. Or check the salad
bar for cut-up fresh pineapple.*

Fruit-and-Chicken Salad

2 cups fresh pineapple chunks (see Tip)
2 ripe nectarines, cut into chunks
1 1/2 Tbsp sugar

DRESSING
   1/4 cup orange juice
   2 Tbsp each cider vinegar and vegetable oil
   1/2 tsp each salt and pepper
6 cups assorted salad greens (about 4 oz)
2 cups cooked chicken chunks
1/2 cup sliced red onion
1/4 cup each chopped mint leaves and toasted pecans

1 Put pineapple and nectarines in a medium bowl; sprinkle with sugar; toss to coat. Let stand 5 minutes until juicy.

2 Meanwhile whisk Dressing ingredients in a large bowl.

3 Add fruit and juices, then remaining ingredients. Toss
to mix and coat.

BLT and Avocado Salad

6 strips bacon

1 ripe avocado

2 medium tomatoes

1 bag (12 oz) American salad mix (a blend of iceberg, romaine, red cabbage, carrots and radishes)

1 can (11 oz) whole kernel corn, drained

1 cup packaged garlic-flavored croutons

1/2 cup bottled ranch dressing

1 Cook bacon as directed on package; drain on paper towels. When cool, break into large pieces.

2 Meanwhile prepare avocado (see Tip) and cut each tomato in 8 wedges.

3 Place in a large bowl, add remaining ingredients except dressing and toss to mix. Add dressing and toss to coat, or arrange salad on plates and drizzle with dressing.

SERVES 4

PER SERVING: 397 cal,
8 g pro, 27 g car, 4 g fiber,
30 g fat (6 g saturated fat),
16 mg chol, 649 mg sod

TIP *Cut avocado in half lengthwise around the seed, then rotate halves to separate. Slide a spoon under the seed and remove. Put halves cut side down, remove skin with fingers and thinly slice each half.*

NOTE *Save the ramen seasoning packets to use in plain
rice and pasta dishes or to
add zest to a vegetable dish.*

TIP *Look for canned stir-fry
vegetables and peanut sauce
in the Asian section of your
food market.*

Warm Asian Ham Salad

1 bunch broccolini (baby broccoli)
8 oz light-and-lean ham, sliced 1/2 in. thick
*3 pkg (3 oz each) ramen noodles, seasoning packages removed
   (see Note)*
*1 can (15 oz) stir-fry mixed vegetables (bean sprouts, bamboo
   shoots, baby corn, water chestnuts), drained (see Tip)*
1/3 cup bottled peanut sauce

1 Bring 3 cups of water to boil in a large covered pot.
Meanwhile cut broccolini crosswise in thirds and ham in
1/2-in. cubes.

2 Break noodles into pot and stir. Stir in broccolini.

3 Cover pot; return to a boil and cook 5 minutes, stirring occasionally. Stir in ham, vegetables and peanut sauce;
cover and cook 1 minute or until heated through.

Warm Spinach-and-Bacon Salad

5 slices (4 oz) Canadian bacon, cut in 1/4-in.-wide
   strips (3/4 cup)
1 medium red onion, thinly sliced and separated in rings
1/4 cup olive oil, preferably extra-virgin
1 bag (10 oz) fresh prewashed spinach
1 can (16 oz) red kidney beans, drained and rinsed
3 Tbsp balsamic vinegar
1/2 tsp each salt and pepper
ACCOMPANIMENT: microwave-cooked potatoes or crusty bread

1 Put Canadian-bacon strips, onion rings and olive oil in
a medium-size skillet. Cook over high heat, stirring often, 3
to 4 minutes until bacon is hot and onion starts to soften.

2 Meanwhile put spinach and beans in a serving bowl.

3 Stir vinegar, salt and pepper into skillet mixture. Bring
to a boil. Pour over spinach mixture; toss to mix and coat.

SERVES 4

PER SERVING: 279 cal,
   14 g pro, 20 g car, 7 g fiber,
   17 g fat (3 g saturated fat),
   14 mg chol, 891 mg sod

SERVES 4

PER SERVING: 399 cal,
  26 g pro, 12 g car, 2 g fiber,
  28 g fat (9 g saturated fat),
  65 mg chol, 1,330 mg sod

NOTE *You can substitute other deli meats and bagged salad.*

DOUBLE UP

Prepare salad greens for several days. Wash greens, drain well and pat dry with paper towels. Refrigerate with paper towels (to absorb moisture) in a plastic bag, crisper or covered container.

Chef's Salad

4 oz each sliced turkey, ham, roast beef and Swiss cheese
1 small cucumber
2 plum tomatoes (such as Roma)
1 bag (12 oz) American salad mix (iceberg lettuce, romaine lettuce, red cabbage, carrots and radishes)
1/2 cup bottled Russian, Thousand Island or ranch dressing

1 Stack turkey and cut in narrow strips. Repeat with ham, roast beef and Swiss cheese. Slice cucumber; cut tomatoes in wedges.

2 Place lettuce and some cucumber slices and tomato wedges in serving bowl or on a platter. Top with turkey, ham, roast beef, cheese and remaining cucumber and tomatoes. Serve with dressing.

SERVES 6

PER SERVING: 210 cal,
  22 g pro, 13 g car, 2 g fiber,
  8 g fat (2 g saturated fat),
  54 mg chol, 265 mg sod

PREPARING A FRESH MANGO

STEP 1 *Holding mango on a cutting board, cut a single slice along each side of the long flat seed so you have two halves.*

STEP 2 *Holding the peel side of one half on a cutting board, score the flesh of the mango lengthwise, then crosswise, being careful not to cut through the peel.*

STEP 3 *Bend the scored portion backward, then cut along the peel to loosen cubed fruit. Cut peel off the fruit remaining on seed. Carefully cut off flesh, then dice.*

Turkey-Mango Salad

DRESSING
  1/2 tsp freshly grated lime peel
  1/4 cup lime juice
  2 Tbsp vegetable oil
  1 Tbsp honey
  1 1/2 tsp grated fresh ginger
  1/2 tsp salt
  1/8 tsp ground red pepper (cayenne)
3 cups diced roast turkey
1 mango (see Preparing a Fresh Mango), halved and diced
1 cup strawberries, hulled and cut in quarters
2 scallions, sliced diagonally
2 cups each shredded spinach and iceberg lettuce
GARNISH: small spinach leaves

1 Whisk Dressing ingredients in a large bowl until blended.

2 Add turkey, mango, strawberries and scallions. Stir to coat. Add shredded spinach and lettuce. Toss to mix.

3 Line platter or individual plates with spinach leaves. Top with turkey mixture.

STEP 1

STEP 2

STEP 3

Index of Ingredients

Photo credits

Cover: Charles Schiller; p. 8: Sang An; p. 11: Rita Maas; p. 12: Alison Miksch; p. 15: Jeff McNamara; pp. 16, 19, 20: John Uher; p. 22: Charles Schiller; p. 26: Jeff McNamara; p. 29: Charles Schiller; p. 30: Jacqueline Hopkins; p. 33: John Uher; p. 34: Jacqueline Hopkins; p. 37: Charles Schiller; pp. 38, 41: Jacqueline Hopkins; p. 43: John Uher; p. 44: Mark Thomas; pp. 47, 48, 51: John Uher; p. 52: Charles Schiller; p. 53: Jacqueline Hopkins; pp. 54, 56, 59, 60: John Uher; p. 63: Mark Ferri; p. 65: Jacqueline Hopkins; pp. 67, 68: Charles Schiller; pp. 71, 72, 75: John Uher; pp. 76, 79: Charles Schiller; pp. 81, 82, 85: John Uher; p. 86: Mark Ferri; p. 89: Mark Thomas; p. 90: Jacqueline Hopkins; p. 93: Charles Schiller; p. 94: Jacqueline Hopkins; p. 93: Charles Schiller; p. 94: Jacqueline Hopkins; p. 97: Jeff McNamara; pp. 98, 101, 102: John Uher; p. 104, 107: Jacqueline Hopkins; pp. 108, 110: Charles Schiller; p. 113: Jacqueline Hopkins; p. 114: Sang An; p. 117: Jacqueline Hopkins; p. 118: John Uher; p. 121: Sang An; p. 123: John Uher; back cover, clockwise from top left: Charles Schiller; John Uher; Sang An; Sang An.

Acknowledgments

The publisher wishes to thank Jane Chesnutt; Ellen R. Greene, Nancy dell'Aria, Mary Ellen Banashek, Marisol Vera, Sue Kakstys, Michele Fedele, Robb Riedel, Kim Walker, Greg Robertson, Margaret T. Farley; Cathy Dorsey; and all the photographers whose images are reproduced in the book.

Recipe page 35 by Michael Lomonaco.